# Halloween

## By Trudi Strain Trueit

**Reading Consultant**
Cecilia Minden-Cupp, PhD
Former Director of the Language and Literacy Program
Harvard Graduate School of Education
Cambridge, Massachusetts

Children's Press®
A Division of Scholastic Inc.
New York  Toronto  London  Auckland  Sydney
Mexico City  New Delhi  Hong Kong
Danbury, Connecticut

Designer: Herman Adler
Photo Researcher: Caroline Anderson
The photo on the cover shows a young girl ready for a Halloween party.

**Library of Congress Cataloging-in-Publication Data**

Trueit, Trudi Strain.
  Halloween / by Trudi Strain Trueit.
      p. cm. — (Rookie read-about holidays)
  ISBN-10: 0-531-12456-8 (lib. bdg.)          0-531-11837-1 (pbk.)
  ISBN-13: 978-0-531-12456-7 (lib. bdg.)      978-0-531-11837-5 (pbk.)
  1. Halloween—Juvenile literature. I. Title. II. Series.
  GT4965.T78 2006
  394.2646—dc22                                    2006003956

CHILDREN'S PRESS, and ROOKIE READ-ABOUT®, and associated
logos are trademarks and/or registered trademarks of Scholastic Library
Publishing. SCHOLASTIC and associated logos are trademarks and/or
registered trademarks of Scholastic Inc.
1 2 3 4 5 6 7 8 9 10 R 16 15 14 13 12 11 10 09 08 07

It is Halloween night. Are you scared of ghosts and goblins? Are you excited by costumes and candy? Maybe you are feeling a little of both!

The Celts (KELTS) lived in Western Europe about two thousand years ago. They thought that the spirits of dead people came back to life on October 31st.

The remains of a Celtic house in Scotland

# October 2007

| Sunday | Monday | Tuesday | Wednesday | Thursday | Friday | Saturday |
|--------|--------|---------|-----------|----------|--------|----------|
|        | 1      | 2       | 3         | 4        | 5      | 6        |
| 7      | 8      | 9       | 10        | 11       | 12     | 13       |
| 14     | 15     | 16      | 17        | 18       | 19     | 20       |
| 21     | 22     | 23      | 24        | 25       | 26     | 27       |
| 28     | 29     | 30      | 31        |          |        |          |

The Celts put out food and
drinks to welcome
the ghosts. They also lit
bonfires, danced, and dressed
in costumes.

As time passed, October 31
became known as Halloween.

The custom of carving pumpkins into jack-o'-lanterns comes from an Irish folktale. (The Irish are relatives of the Celts.) The folktale is about a man named Jack.

An arrangement of jack-o'-lanterns

The Irish once used turnips to carve
jack-o'-lanterns.

Everyone thought Jack was a mean man. When Jack died, he was doomed to haunt the Earth forever. His only light was a hollow turnip with a candle inside.

The Irish carved their own turnip jack-o'-lanterns on Halloween to keep Jack away.

The Irish brought their Halloween traditions with them when they came to North America. Pumpkins were easier to carve than turnips, though, so people began using them instead.

Carving a pumpkin

13

Children playing a prank by scaring an adult on Halloween

Playing pranks, or tricks, eventually became part of the Halloween celebration in North America.

Children began the trick-or-treat tradition in the United States in the early 1900s. They went door-to-door and asked people to give them treats. In turn, they wouldn't play tricks. They called out, "Trick or treat?" as a playful joke.

Trick-or-treating in England in the 1800s

Trick-or-treating through the neighborhood

# Ways to Celebrate

Most children celebrate
Halloween by dressing
up in costumes. They
trick-or-treat in their
neighborhood. Some kids
collect money instead of
candy. The money goes to
help people in need.

Halloween parties are also popular. Party activities might include bobbing for apples or dipping your hands in monster brains (green gelatin).

Bobbing for apples at a party

Special Halloween treats

It's also fun to make cookies in the shapes of bats, cats, jack-o'-lanterns, and witches.

One tradition is to bake
the seeds from your
carved pumpkin. Sprinkle
the seeds with salt for
a crunchy treat.

Pumpkin seeds

A Halloween scarecrow

Some families decorate
for Halloween. They
hang ghosts made of tissue
paper from trees. They
make scarecrows out
of straw and clothing.

Telling ghost stories is also a Halloween custom. Be careful! It may be hard to fall asleep after listening to all those spooky tales. Boo!

Scared? It is just a story.

# Words You Know

bobbing for apples

carving

costumes

jack-o'-lantern

pumpkin seeds

scarecrow

trick-or-treating

turnips

31

# Index

# About the Author

Trudi Strain Trueit is a former television news reporter and weather forecaster. She has written more than thirty fiction and nonfiction books for children. Ms. Trueit lives near Seattle, Washington, with her husband Bill.

# Photo Credits

Photographs © 2007: Bridgeman Art Library International Ltd., London/New York: 17 (Private Collection/C. Gavin Graham Gallery, London, UK); Corbis Images: 9, 30 bottom right (Philip James Corwin), 13, 30 top right (Jose Luis Pelaez), 22 (PhotoCuisine), 25, 31 top left (TH-Foto/zefa), 29 (Zisch/zefa); Dembinsky Photo Assoc./Michael P. Gadomski: 10, 31 bottom right; Getty Images/Mel Yates/Stone: 3, 30 bottom left; Index Stock Imagery/Mitch Diamond: 26, 31 top right; Mary Evans Picture Library: 14; PhotoEdit/John Neubauer: 21, 30 top left; Superstock, Inc.: 5 (age fotostock), 18, 31 bottom left (Comstock), cover (Richard Heinzen).